THE
Archive Photographs
SERIES

WINCHESTER

FROM THE SOLLARS COLLECTION

A view of the High Street, 1 June 1962.

THE
Archive Photographs
SERIES

WINCHESTER
FROM THE SOLLARS COLLECTION

Compiled by
John Brimfield

CHALFORD

First published 1995
Copyright © John Brimfield, 1995

The Chalford Publishing Company
St Mary's Mill, Chalford,
Stroud, Gloucestershire, GL6 8NX

ISBN 0 7524 0173 4

Typesetting and origination by
The Chalford Publishing Company
Printed in Great Britain by
Redwood Books, Trowbridge

Contents

Introduction   7

1.   People   9

2.   Transport   43

3.   Buildings   59

4.   Cathedral and Close   121

Acknowledgements   128

Born in Winchester on 25 February 1918, Bob Sollars was educated at Western Infants, Hyde Junior School, and finally St Thomas Senior School where he was elected Head Boy and Captain of football and cricket. A keen footballer, he played three times for Winchester City Schoolboys' Football Team in a national contest. He left school in 1932 and started work in the retail trade.

On the outbreak of war in September 1939 he volunteered for the Royal Navy but went into the Royal Marines. He took part in the Battle of Crete in 1941 but was left behind at the excavation beach on the southern shores of Crete and was captured on 1 June. He spent the rest of the War in Austria, Stalag XVIIIA (Wolfesberg). He at last arrived home in May 1945, and was demobbed in December of the same year.

His interest in photography started at an early age, when with a school friend he experimented with developing and printing under a blanket in the living room of his home. He later started to take photography seriously and joined the Winchester Photographic Society of which he was twice President. During the early 1950s he turned professional, taking over an existing business which traded mostly in local and national press photography, later adding commercial and industrial photography to the business. He retired early in 1990. He is married to Margaret; they have three children, Robert, Andrew, and Roberta, and five grandchildren. Andrew Sollars now runs the business, continuing the 'Sollars of Winchester' photographic tradition, and adding picture framing to his already heavy workload.

Introduction

Living in Winchester has been all the richer thanks to the photographs taken by Mr E.A. (Bob) Sollars over the last few decades. So frequently we see photographs of a life long ago, but Bob Sollars's pictures faithfully record a rapidly changing way of life we all knew and can associate with. Through the good offices of John Brimfield, Mr Sollars has generously made available to a wider audience his magnificent archive – thank goodness he did not throw away his negatives when he retired.

Looking at the pictures, one becomes aware of the subtle and brutal changes that have occurred during the latter part of our second Elizabethan age. Our Victorian forefathers, with the coming of mechanisation, cleared and rebuilt vast areas. Sadly, in most cases, only rudimentary records are available, often broad-sweeping views by Francis Frith or Winchester's own Mr Beloe remain. Our age has seen the enormous pressure on private mobility with living in pleasant suburbs and the need to commute to work. Transport demand has caused the demise of many private businesses and properties. The centre of Winchester is now devoid of living accommodation (although this is coming back) and a whole way of life almost untouched for many centuries has gone for ever. Walking to work now usually means a short trot from the office car park. City centre schools have closed and become car parks as the later twentieth-century person enjoys his own door to door mobility.

Bob Sollars has also captured formal Winchester – the opening of the old Assize Courts with the procession of Judges to the Cathedral before the coming of the new Crown Courts in continual session.

To Wintonians, it is often the background that is of the greatest interest, capturing glimpses of shops that are no more, bus companies such as Greyfriars, King Alfred, and Hants & Dorset that have left our streets, and events we have long forgotten about like rent protests, with, again, shops in the background that were once household names, shops like Lipton's, Timothy Whites, and Taylors, etc. High Street names today change so rapidly that sometimes no record of the frontage has been kept. Yet all is not doom! Thanks to the Winchester Preservation Trust, wiser counsels have prevailed.

Looking at Mr Sollars's picture of my own house it is pleasing to think that the dilapidated street frontage lacking porches, and pale yellow bricks, grubby and painted over, has now been restored to something like its 1840 dignity. There is a realisation that we have limited resources and that the best of the old must be complimented by the late twentieth century. Bob Sollars's pictures have captured the end of the old world and the start of the new.

Finally, we must be grateful to John Brimfield for using his expert knowledge of the City, and realising that the Sollars Collection will appeal to a wider readership as part of the social history of Great Britain. 'Photo Sollars Winchester' will still be in demand many years from now to show the way we lived.

C.J. Webb
Chairman, Winchester Heritage Centre
An enterprise of the Winchester Preservation Trust
30–32 Upper Brook Street, Winchester

One

People

The Judge leaves the Law Courts, housed at the Great Hall, 1 November 1953.

The Fire Station children's Christmas party, held on 19 December 1953.

The Co-op Guild children's party, 9 January 1954.

The Gas Company children's party, 4 January 1954. Leaning on the table is Jill Pollard, opposite are John Pollard and David Bishop.

Hyde Girls Club bell ringers with their instructor, Mr J. King, about to be televised for children's television. This photograph was taken on 5 May 1954.

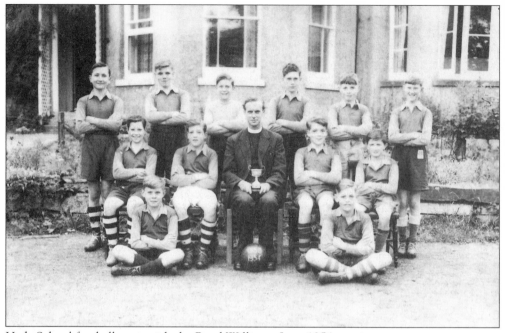

Hyde School football team with the Revd Williams, June 1954.

The Old Contemptibles service at St Thomas' Church, 11 September 1954.

Father Christmas arrives by helicopter with presents from the U.S. Air Force at the Hampshire depot for the children of the Hampshire County Council homes, 21 December 1954.

Mr Cottrill, the local archaeologist, with a skeleton found during excavations at Winnall building site, 8 January 1955.

The Odeon Cinema road safety campaign, 26 February 1955.

The Odeon Cinema children with their Highway Code books, April 1955.

The retirement of Miss E.F. Sivyour from Holy Trinity School, March 1955.

A diver at Durngate during the construction of the new main sewer from Eastgate Street to the new Winnall Housing Estate, April 1955. On the right is Mr A. Stickland – his hourly rate of pay was two shillings.

Mayor D.M. Edmeades visiting North Walls fire station, demonstrating the fire emergency telephone, 28 April 1955.

Mr Peter Smithers campaigning in the Broadway, May 1955.

Hyde Abbey Ladies' Bowling Club, August 1955.

The Royal Naval Association marching down the High Street to the service of the dedication of the new Standard at St John's Church, 18 September 1955.

A service held for the Royal Hampshire Regiment after their passing out parade in Series House gardens, September 1955.

The Mayor, Mrs B.G. Thackery, visiting the Royal Observer Corps, 18 November 1955.

Winchester Cathedral Bell Ringers being visited by the Mayor and Mr and Mrs Peter Smithers on 13 December 1955.

Marks & Spencer staff Christmas party held on 22 December 1955. Fifth and sixth on the left are Mrs Banning and Mrs Smith. Second from the left, standing at the back, is Mrs Flux.

Old folks' party at Sparsholt village hall, 3 January 1956. Front row: (left to right) Mrs Kimber, Mr Kimber, Mr Maundrel (Vicar), Mr Merwood and Mrs Bayford.

Hants & Dorset bus station children's party in the Guildhall, January 1956.

The boxer Joe Dumper training at Royal Green Jackets gymnasium with Mr A. Cozens in March 1956.

The Mayor visiting the Sea Cadet Corps at training ship *Itchen*, Parchment Street, 20 March 1956.

Circus elephants arriving at Winchester railway station, 27 June 1956.

West Hill Cricket Club, photographed on 18 August 1956. Front row: (left to right) Mr Ship, Mr Bull and Mr Lucas; on the back row, fifth from left, is Mr Strange.

Wilfred Pickles at the Willow Tree Inn on 14 October 1956, about to push over the column of pennies. Also present is the Mayor, Mr P. Woodhouse.

Brown & Harrisons' Dairy Ltd children's party, 10 January 1957.

An interior view of the West of England Sack Factory at Bar End and some of the staff, 19 February 1957.

Inspection of the St John's Ambulance cadets, 21 March 1957.

Staff of the West of England Sack factory at Bar End Road, now the site of the Hampshire County Council supplies depot, photographed on 10 April 1957.

Mr Charles Mann, the City of Winchester mace bearer, photographed on 10 July 1957.

Brown and Harrisons' Dairy children's Christmas party, 1 January 1958.

The Post Office children's Christmas party, 4 January 1958.

The Police receive their new badge and helmet, March 1958.

After being presented with their new badge and helmet in March, the Police received a new mode of transport, on 18 December 1958.

County High School prefects, 4 June 1958.

Mr W. Goodchild, street cleaner, at work in North Walls on 4 February 1960. Note the two-way traffic before the coming of the one-way system.

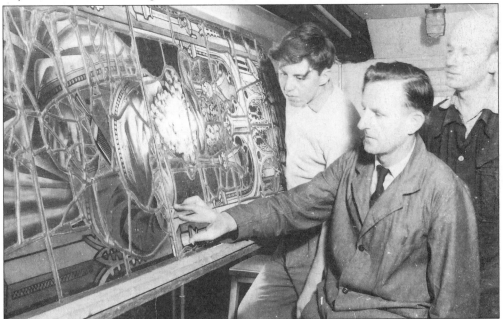

The staff of Mortons' Glass Works in St Swithun Street, working on a stained glass leaded window, 12 May 1960.

The 'Penguins' swimming gala at the Lido, 21 July 1960.

The Army Cadet Force in Middle Brook Street central car park, September 1960. The building on the left was Harman & Co., the rag and bone store.

All Saints' School football team
with Mr Lewington (on the left),
March 1961.

An interior view of Worthy Down
signal box, 28 October 1961.

The collection point for the Mile of Pennies outside St Peter's Church, December 1962.

Staff being collected for the Brown and Harrison's Dairy staff outing at the Cart and Horses Inn, Kingsworthy, in May 1963.

In May 1964, a protest against hanging took place outside Winchester Prison. Note the old pedestrian entrance opposite St James Lane.

The Ballards of Winnall football team as it was in May 1964. Back row: (from third left) Mr Tracey, Mr Pink, Mr Budgen, and Mr Whitcher. In the front row on the left is Mr Ballard; also pictured are Mr Dumper, Mr Foulds, Mr Carter, and Mr Ivory.

Mrs M. Palmer receiving a cheque from a bingo caller in August 1964. From left to right: Mr M. Fletcher, Mrs D. Smith, and Ritz manager Mr J. Pitt.

Mr A. Phillis, a watch and clock maker, attending to the clock at Lloyds Bank, September 1964.

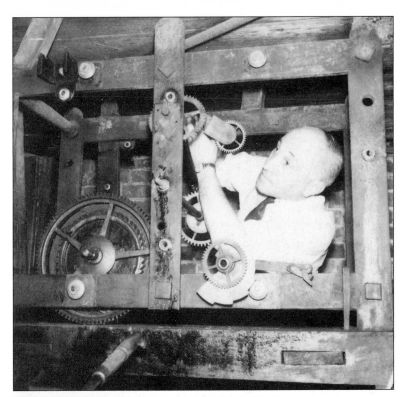

Mr Phillis working on the clock mechanism.

Mr L.G.L. Chew, the City Champion, receives a savings challenge from the Mayor of Salisbury, Councillor W.S. Biddle, on behalf of the Mayor of Winchester, Mrs B. Carpenter Turner, in October 1966.

The Winchester and District Cub Scouts marching on the St George's Day parade, 28 April 1968.

Field Marshal Lord Montgomery of Alamein addressing pupils after the official renaming of the school, June 1968.

These members of King Alfred Boys' Club are 'kidnapping' Mr Ken Wapshire, the proprietor of Ken's Fish and Chip Shop (26 October 1968).

The Mayor, Alderman S.G. Steel, proclaims the dissolution of Parliament from the steps of the City Cross, May 1970.

Mr Abrahams, manager of the Lido swimming pool, pictured in September 1971.

The last sessions of the Magistrates' Court in the Guildhall, February 1972.

A protest march held by Winchester tenants against rent increases, May 1972.

Pickets in the High Street, September 1972. These workmen, employed on the construction of the new Law Courts, were on strike for a guaranteed weekly wage of £30. In view on the right is the Old Holm Oak Tree.

One of the hobbies on display in an exhibition held at the Guildhall in December 1972, with the Mayor and Mr Foot of the Rotary Club and Mr W. Eyles.

The firemen's strike of May 1977. These pickets are outside the Hampshire County Council offices in Romsey Road.

The Mayor, Mr David G. Ball, holds a party under the Pentice for Winchester old age pensioners to commemorate the Queen's Silver Jubilee in June 1977.

Sign-writer Mr Thompson re-writes the names of Winchester's parliamentary representatives on the wall of the Great Hall.

A memorial to Mr Douglas Bylett in the High Street, outside Lloyds Bank. This was removed on Sunday 18 May 1980, soon after this picture was taken.

Two

Transport

The Hampshire County Council's first mobile library van was a specially designed Bedford built to carry 1850 books. It was officially opened by Sir Charles Chute, Bart., M.C., Chairman of Hampshire County Council, in July 1953.

This accident at Stockbridge Road railway bridge took place on 3 June 1954.

An Anglo-American vintage car rally passes through the city, 10 September 1954.

Moorside Motor Works in Union Street, August 1955.

The showrooms of Wessex Motors in St Cross Road, April 1956.

The Winchester by-pass photographed on 30 April 1958. Also in the view is Spitfire Bridge.

Mr R. Johnson, fruit and vegetable merchant of Lower Brook Street, photographed on 12 July 1958.

A 'Red Rover' stage coach at the India Arms on 9 September 1958.

The new Bull Bros motor workshop at Winnall (late of Cossack Lane), 19 December 1958. After this, their old premises were occupied by T.A. Hutchinson, builder.

A fleet of new cars for Richardson & Starling Ltd of Hyde Street, 1 January 1959.

An accident at Weeke Pond, 9 January 1959. Note the old Police box on the left.

Mr H.L. Bradley's garage in Staple Gardens, May 1961.

Mr Charles Salter's new 'Caterer's' van seen in Eastgate Street in February 1962.

A view of the central car park, now the Brooks Centre, 1 June 1962.

The entrance to the central car park and a row of four shops on the right-hand side, June 1962.

An accident near Whitchurch involving a King Alfred bus, which took place in December 1962.

An accident in St John's Street, September 1964.

A Camill dumper manufactured by Campbell & McGill Engineering of Winnall, April 1965.

Another accident involving a King Alfred bus, this time at the junction of Chilbolton Avenue and Stockbridge Road, April 1965. This bus, which spent some time in America, was recently purchased and returned to Winchester.

Part of the Will Short Ltd garage showrooms in St Cross Road, May 1965. Note, on the right-hand side, the start of the demolition of Hooper & Ashby Ltd, builders' merchants.

H.J. Coombes & Co. Ltd of Andover Road, May 1965.

The Market Service Station, Andover Road, May 1965.

A large load travelling north on the south-bound lane of the by-pass after leaving the Petersfield Road. October 1966.

The same large load crossing over to the north-bound lane at Winnall cross roads, by Wadham's Garage.

A general view of the High Street as it looked in August 1967. Then, traffic used to enter the High Street from Little Minster Street.

The Airlie Road corner in December 1968, with Winchester City Association Football Club ground. The Club was founded in 1884.

The official opening of the Bar End flyover in August 1973. The ceremony was performed by the Mayoress, Mrs C.A. Taylor.

The Bar End junction, August 1973. Note the police and contractors ready to close the central reservation and Morstead Road.

Weekes Garage/Lewtas Motors. The price of petrol was 72p and 74p a gallon. July 1978.

A motor cycle demonstration in the city in March 1979. The demonstrators were protesting against the wearing of crash helmets. They are seen here entering Andover Road.

Three
Buildings

During excavations on the corner of Middle Brook Street and St George's Street, a Roman mosaic was found. This picture was taken on 1 September 1953.

This picture, dated 14 November 1953, shows the high price of new laid eggs, 5s. 6d. or 5s. 9d. a dozen – for some, nearly twice the hourly rate of pay!

A snow scene in Sussex Street (City Road end), January 1954.

The junction of Chesil Street and Bridge Street, January 1954. The end building in Bridge Street is Ken's Fish and Chip Shop before it moved to its new location on the corner of St John's Street.

Winnall Industrial Estate, showing Curtis & Padwick, 6 August 1954.

Westcombe Motors pictured on 1 December 1954 after it had collapsed in City Road. Behind the trees is the Hermit's Tower.

Union Street from North Walls on 22 February 1955. The buildings on the right of the picture have since all been demolished. Note the metal dustbins!

The interior of Ponsford's Bakery in North Walls as it appeared in February 1955.

The Co-op bakery and staff, February 1955. Pictured are: (left to right) Mr Mumford, Mr Mumford, Mr Shepherd, Mr Saunders, Mr Habgood, and Mr Dillow.

The demolition of houses in North Walls, 28 April 1955.

The Post Office Tavern in Parchment Street, 27 November 1955. On the right is J. Stone, gents' hairdressers.

The mayor visiting R.H.C.H. hut wards during Christmas 1955.

The St George & The Dragon leaded light above the front entrance door to the George Hotel, March 1956.

The St George's Street and Jewry Street corner during demolition, 15 March 1956.

The top of St George's Street, 15 March 1956. The first building on the left is Kingdons. Also in the picture is the City Tavern. Note the pedestrian walkway from the garage to the hotel.

An interior view of the Cadena Cafe (now the Baker's Oven), photographed on 14 November 1956.

The Queen's Head, Upper Brook Street, 20 June 1957.

Will Short's Ltd, Southgate Street, 11 September 1957. The white house was later demolished
The building next door is Crosby's sports shop.

Father Christmas arriving in a 1903 Humber at Sherriff and Ward on 23 November 1953.

Morris dancers in Castle Yard, 21 July 1958.

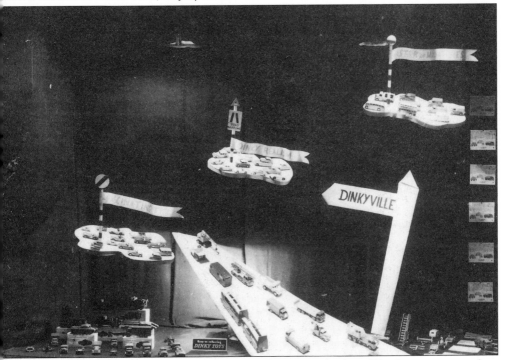

Hollands' shop window in the Upper High Street showing a display of Dinky toys, pictured on 21 July 1958.

The south corner of Colebrook Street looking from the Cathedral, 10 October 1958. At the top, in the centre, is the playground of St Mary's School.

A display of Brazil's pies, 21 January 1959, in Hubert Smith's shop in the City Road. The pies cost 2s. 8d. and 3s. each.

The demolition of the gasometer in Andover Road, 20 March 1959. The gasometer had been constructed in 1856. Gas lighting was introduced to the High Street in 1832, and in 1834 it was extended to the whole city.

The interior of Mr S. Offord's shop at 77 North Walls, opposite Hyde Abbey Road. The date is 1 May 1959, Rowntree's fruit gums cost 3d., Cadbury's Roses 1s. 1d. per quarter, and Nutty Nutty sweets are 7d. per quarter.

The new Hampshire County Council offices, 11 May 1959.

The K.R.R.C. advertising a film at the Odeon on 15 May 1959.

The B.P. drilling rig at Chilcombe, 14 November 1959. The rig was test drilling to assess the possibility of gas storage underground over an area of 3500 acres.

Woolford & Sons, builders, at Bar End Road, November 1959.

Hyde Street looking south, March 1960, and (below) looking north.

In this picture dating from March 1960 we are looking at the Post Office Engineers entrance and Hyde Abbey Motor Works. The houses in the foreground were demolished to make way for petrol pumps and car showrooms.

The entrance to Hyde Abbey Motors showing workshops and petrol pumps, March 1960.

Do you remember the High Street as it looked in 1960? This and the following set of seventeen pictures were all taken on the same day, 25 July 1960. Shown here is Plummers.

Hepworth's.

Heming & Tudor.

Allen's.

Liptons.

T. Walton.

Burtons.

Hayter's.

Dowlings.

Wymans.

John Collier.

New Bell & Crown.

Currys.

Home & Colonial.

Dunn's.

Sherriff & Ward's.

Hutchins.

Churchill's.

Pictured here in July 1960, the Mercantile Store's last day of trading was 17 September of that year.

Luck's the chemist in Southgate Street. The date is 29 September 1960, and Miss Dorothy Gain is receiving her £100 prize from the Sebbix Shampoo manager. On the left is Mr E. Luck.

Trod Smith's building being converted into Jaeger's, 25 October 1960. On the right is the Wimpy Bar.

The Awdry Tea Rooms which used to be above W.H. Smith & Sons in the High Street. This was one of only six Awdry tea rooms; the other five were in Bournemouth, Darlington, Durham, Brussels, and Paris.

The interior of Hutchins sweet shop, May 1960. This now forms part of the Blue Dolphin Fish Restaurant.

The Mayor of Winchester, Councillor Lt Col. D.C. Spelman, who officially opened the Old Chesil Rectory after it had undergone extensive renovations. With the Mayor is Councillor Stanley Steel. (19 May 1961).

The arrival of the Bishop of Winchester, Dr A.T.P. Williams, for the dedication of St Luke's Church on 12 July 1961.

The Square as it looked on 16 September 1961. E.J. Hibberd was the last umbrella repair shop in the city.

The Square, 16 September 1961.

The Bull Drove swimming pool in Garnier Road in 1961. The caretaker at that time was Mr Ted Wilkins.

Pearson's salerooms in Tower Road (the five corners), 11 December 1961.

After a lightning strike on the gable end of a house in Canute Road, January 1962.

The Mercantile
Stores under
demolition. The
last day trading
was 17 September
1960. This
photograph was
taken in February
1962.

The foundations of
the Wessex Hotel,
built by Drewitts,
pictured on 1 June
1962.

Boundary Street looking towards Eastgate Street, August 1963. Numbers 1–7 are still standing.

Boundary Street looking looking west. On the right-hand is Tagart, Morgan and Coles, timber importers, August 1963.

Friarsgate looking east in June 1964. The Greyfriars flats are under construction.

Friarsgate looking towards the central car park, June 1964

Hancock's staff and their vans. This picture was taken on 19 December 1964 in Park Avenue on the parade ground of the A.T.C. Third from the left is Mr Hayward; next is Mr Pickett; and last in the line, on the right, is Mr Burgess.

A fire above the Theatre Royal bar on 20 January 1965.

The remains of the old Law Courts as they looked in March 1965. The Law Courts had been demolished in 1937 due to subsidence.

The Goodyear Tyre Co. in Victoria Road.

Weapons in the cells of North Walls police station, handed in during a firearms amnesty in November 1965.

A Round Table bonfire night procession through the Broadway, November 1965.

Tower Street, January 1966. On the left is the construction site of the multi-storey car park.

The corner of Jewry Street, January 1966.

The fire at
Teague and
King's, 18 Little
Minster Street,
which struck in
February 1966.

H.R.H. Princess Margaret opened the new Police Headquarters in October 1966. Here we see the March Past by the Special Constables.

The Old Blue Boar Inn, hit by a gib of Caswell Cranes of Winnall, October 1966.

Edwin Carter's, builders, loading up the new bank counter top, October 1966.

The counter top going into Portsmouth Trustee Savings Bank on the Jewry Street/St George's Street corner.

A tank in the Broadway in April 1967. On the right-hand side is the King Alfred snack bar.

Dick's on the Silver Hill/Cross Keys Passage corner. This is now Hunts the Chemist. December 1967.

The Abbey gardens as they looked on 6 March 1968.

Lower Moors Road on the Winnall Industrial Estate in April 1968.

Southgate Street, 27
June 1968.

Andover Road Cattle
Market, August 1968.

A fire at the Guildhall on 28 April 1969. Note the holes in the firemen's hose!

Winton Court Hotel, Southgate Street, pictured in October 1969.

The interior of the Georgian Restaurant in Jewry Street in November 1969.

Rivers Engineering Co., Winnall, March 1970.

The old G.P.O. sorting desk, April 1970.

The new Council Offices under construction in Colebrook Street, January 1970.

The opening of the new Council Offices by the Mayor, July 1970.

St Cross Road showing Newton's Nurseries on the left, September 1972.

The old Market Inn and G.H. Bell, September 1972.

The Castle Hotel, October 1972.

Post Office Telephone Engineers, 75 Hyde Street, January 1973.

The Odeon Cinema,
February 1973.

Lord Hailsham
opening the
new Law
Courts, 22
February 1974.

The Georgian Restaurant in Jewry Street, June 1973.

North Walls shops, October 1974.

The north side of City Road (above) and the south side (below), August 1975.

The view up Andover Road, August 1975.

The corner of Sussex Street in August 1975, before road widening.

Mr Mike Shannon of Southampton and England football teams, opening Milletts' new shop in September 1975.

Chesil Street looking from East Hill corner in September 1975.

River cleaning in the park, with the classrooms of Danemark School in view in the background. October 1975.

Jewry Street in October 1978.

The last of Colson Road in July 1980.

The Theatre Royal in August 1981, before redecoration.

Four
Cathedral and Close

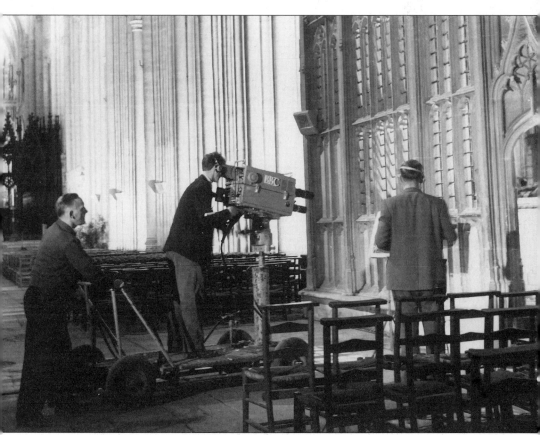

A television camera in action, broadcasting from the Cathedral on 26 November 1954. The Dean of Winchester, The Very Revd Dr E.G. Selwyn, gave the commentary. The programme was also broadcast to viewers in France.

The Judges' Sunday procession to the Cathedral, 13 May 1955.

The Hampshire Carabiniers Yeomanry Guidon in Winchester Cathedral on Sunday morning 6 November 1955, prior to it being laid up. Either side of Sir Dymoke White, the Honorary Colonel, are Colonel J.F.N. Baxendale, Lieutenant-Colonel J.P. Purvis, and Major A.K. Freeman. With the standard is Captain P.W. Ryan, and his escorts are B.S.M. Pearce and B.S.M. Brimfield.

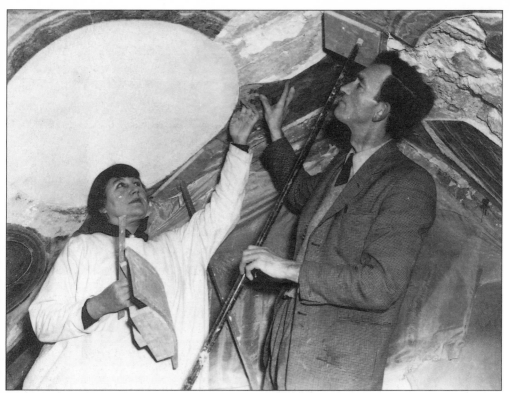

Restoration work under the vault of the Guardian Angel Chapel, 31 December 1957. The work was carried out by Professor and Mrs R.W. Baker of the Royal College of Art.

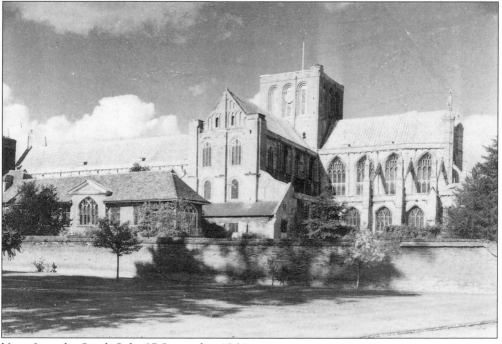

View from the South Side, 27 September 1964.

Cathedral pillars under repair, January 1965.

Excavations on the North Side of the Cathedral, October 1965.

The Archbishop of Canterbury, The Most Revd Michael Ramsey, blessing the congregation from the Shrine of St Swithun at the Patronal Festival in the Cathedral, which took place in July 1966. The congregation numbered three thousand.

The Vienna Boys' Choir photographed in Winchester Cathedral, March 1971.

The Judges drive to court in horse and carriage (1974).

The enthronement of a new Bishop of Winchester, The Rt Revd John Taylor, on 8 February 1975. Pictured are: (left to right) The Dean of Winchester, The Very Revd Michael Stancliffe; The Archbishop of Canterbury, The Most Revd Donald Coggan; and The Bishop of Winchester.

The restoration of Pilgrims Hall, in a photograph taken on 3 March 1959. In the centre at the front is Mr J. Bass, and on the right at the front is Mr A. Trueman, the general foreman.

This medieval dinner was held in Pilgrims Hall in November 1969 in aid of the Cancer Relief Fund. Note the timber frame of the Hall.

The St Cross Dole, the porter to the Lodge, Mr E.A. Sollars, and a visitor. September 1969.

Acknowledgements

The author would like to thank the following people and organisations for their help with the compilation of the book, which is, above all, an endeavour to stir memories of the not too distant past for the reader.

First and foremost, thanks to Mr E.A. (Bob) Sollars for allowing access to the remaining stock of nearly 20,000 sets of negatives from where all the pictures in this publication come. They all carry the credit line 'Photo Sollars Winchester'. Also to the darkroom technician Mr L. Mears, who has printed all the negatives in this book, and the Wintonians who have helped with the information – Mr A. Stickland, Mr A. Brown, Mr A. Brooks, Mr C. Webb, Mr B. Whitcher, Mr J. Hyde, Mrs D. Thompson, and Mr L. Miles. To the Hampshire County Library, especially Mrs P. Stevens and the staff of the Local Studies Department for their help with the *Hampshire Chronicle* files and the loan of fifteen negatives from their collection of photographs from the Sollars Collection. Thanks also to the Curator of Winchester Cathedral.

I would like to offer a tribute also to my wife, Jennifer, for her endless patience and co-operation over the last two years; and to my sons, Robert, with his typing skills, and Julian, for his help with the computer programming.

And not forgetting the Winchester Heritage Centre, where in time there will be an even greater collection of photographs thanks to Bob Sollars.